Securing the Perimeter

Poems by
Elaine Handley

Clare Songbirds Publishing House Chapbook Series
ISBN 978-1-947653-17-7
Clare Songbirds Publishing House
Securing the Perimeter © 2018 Elaine Handley
All Rights Reserved. Clare Songbirds Publishing House retains right to reprint.

Permission to reprint individual poems must be obtained from the author who owns the copyright.

Printed in the United States of America
FIRST EDITION

Clare Songbirds Publishing House Mission Statement:
Clare Songbirds Publishing House was established to provide a print forum for the creation of limited edition, fine art from poets and writers, both established and emerging. We strive to reignite and continue a tradition of quality, accessible literary arts to the national and international community of writers, and readers. Chapbook manuscripts are carefully chosen for their ability to propel the expansion of art and ideas in literary form. We provide an accessible way to promote the art of words in order to resonate with, and impact, readers not yet familiar with the siren song of poets and writers. Clare Songbirds Publishing House espouses a singular cultural development where poetry creates community and becomes commonplace in public places.

Clare Songbirds Publishing House
140 Cottage Street
Auburn, New York 13021
www.ClareSongbirdspub.com

Contents

Open Circle	7
Nightwatch	8
Afterburn	9
Insomniac's Prayer	10
Unmanned	11
Turn Sideways	12
Letter to My Father	13
Dedication of the Vietnam Memorial	14
Christmas Eve 1983 at the Vietnam Memorial	15
Like Grief	16
Armour	17
Chicken Love	18
For Soldier Returning	19
Securing the Perimeter	20
Recovery	22
No Blood	23
Civil War Greece	24
Memoir	25
Toward a War Poem	26
Kisses	27
The Frail Ones	28
At the Airport	29
Matrilineal	30
Rapprochement	31
Requiem for the Living	32
Patrilineal	33
Praise Song	34
Walking at Dusk on New Year's Eve	35

Acknowledgements

Grateful acknowledgement is made to the editors of the following journals and anthology in which these poems have appeared:

Athena: "Night Watch"

Aurorean: "Patrilineal"

Cactus Heart: "Chicken Love"

Ekphrasis: "Orant" (now "Praise Song")

Like Light: 25 Years of Poetry & Prose by Bright Hill Poets & Writers: "Memoir"

The Lucid Stone: "Dedication of the Vietnam Memorial"

Numero Cinq: "Open Circle," "Securing the Perimeter," "Rapprochement"

Cover art by Marco Montanari: "Dismantled to the Blood Moon" painted in response to the poem "Securing the Perimeter."

Author photo courtesy of stockstudiophotography.com © 2011
No images are in the public domain.
Any unauthorized use subject to triple fees and federal fines.
All images copyright 2011

For Isaac

As the area of light expands, so does the perimeter of darkness.

~Albert Einstein

Open Circle

After every war
someone's got to tidy up.
Things won't pick
themselves up, after all.
            from *The End and The Beginning*
            by Wislawa Symborska

Women have done it throughout time,
quietly undertaking repairs.
First they solder together
circuits broken in themselves.
Hard to do and clumsy; sometimes
they give up and make do. Jagged
fragments float in the bloodstream,
lodging close to the skin.

Next, they have to cauterize time.
When he returns it must be as if
no one has changed, no feelings
clotted. She must know him even though
he is now a stranger
in the wreckage of the familiar.
She watches him on the lip
of a tunnel looking
for passage from war to her.

It is the bottom of the morning
in their lives, lonesome and surviving
on memories and dreams
they wrote each other. She has tried
to tidy up, she knows things now
she didn't know before:
they have amputated children,
they live like ghosts.

The truth is not hers to utter,
but there is no one else to say it.

Night Watch

You clutch for some weapon
and find me stiff and awake watching
your old wounds bleed sweat.

Your hot metallic dreams rip
open my sleep. Stunned by the decay,
wide-eyed as the dead
I don't know how to protect you.

I never wanted to know
the meaning of the ace of spades
or hump the Ho Chi Minh Trail with you.

I believed our terrain
to be less dangerous--the way
open and clean. No traps, no bodies
without names, leaves still on the trees.

Love is an infiltration; time only for panic.
And you cannot be saved. For I am one
more friend dying in your arms.

AFTERBURN

On TV the towers
disintegrated with grace.

The sick truth
registered first in the gut
then gurgled up to the brain.

The leaping ended:
in rubble of bone dust
the ashy wind
the empty
blue sky.

Insomniac's Prayer

Stranded in forever night
on a patient bed of nails
with the prick and bleed
of thoughts that will not leave.

Still and silent, your oblivious warmth
anchors me here
where my vigilance ripens to ache,
my shadowed self rusts.

I listen to the creak and groan of mistakes
trying to take flight in their bloated state.
I worry the next day into litany.

This blue daze of wakefulness,
its scaly endurance, purgatory
of the living, hair shirt
of the mind—
Deliver me.
Deliver me.

Unmanned

You tell me how
sins line up obedient to memory
and file by, carefully saluting you--
their lone commander.
Too much to secure, watch
for, protect and no time to rest.
The weapons you won't set down
chopped apart, *Guernica* -like
in your black and white
rendition of our life.

Kaleidioscoped, you make strange shapes
and colors brighten and fade.

And sometimes you disappear right
when I am looking at you.

Turn Sideways

For David Wheeler

to the storm
tuck yourself into
it
patiently wait
for the onslaught
to pass
take the time to absorb
Time
and all its warriors
will be unable
to see you
waiting
where the wind
flies around you
and the snow
conceals your tracks
and turns you into
one crystal
of light.

Letter to My Father

When you were drifting off to sleep,
in idle moments, did you think of me?
Did you remember my eyes, neither yours
nor my mothers, or my face?
The old pictures show what a strange child I was
too sad, too pensive.
Did you know what to see in me?

The years between, some kind of waiting room:
awful décor and empty, purgatory
with not enough chairs
and no one calling my name. Lost is lost,
missing is lost, lost is missing what you need.

After you died, I thought you would hover near,
so we could come to an understanding.
Instead, days were wrapped in wool,
breathing shallow the flat air.
No dream visitations, no signs or spirit rapping.
You were more lost to me than before; the ordinary
fact that my father was dead was all I had.

Who doesn't ruminate on dead parents?
Whose orphaning isn't profound, even if it happened
long before death? All I can do
is stitch together yet another poem
about a dead father, which the world does not need.
But memory is a needle that pierces,
longing a thread for suturing words and memories,
uneven and crooked,
a scar you could recognize me by.

Dedication of the Vietnam Memorial

November 1982

A woman knowing no one
name to seek out, to touch,
clasps her man's hand.
Suddenly his face crumbles
as he turns from her.
How can he explain
that he has known death
more intimately
than he has known her?
That he scattered desire
with the medals
he threw away
in the jungle?

No war ends.
Men stalk themselves
for years
in silent waves of names.

Christmas Eve 1982:
At the Vietnam Memorial

I am not sure why
I wanted to be there that night.
All of D.C. seemed empty—
no one on the streets, barely
any traffic, just a handful
of vets keeping a kind of vigil going:
a few candles, hushed voices.
Dedicated just a month before
in sunlight: my reflection held
names of the dead inside my body.

I couldn't figure out why
they were so sad, these wings
of granite with names.
And that night sadder still
in the dark, hollow city
where old men scheme
young men into war.

I was looking
for you, even though
you were there with me.
You, who told me
about the rancid stench
of death you ate
for a week
after you killed
the first time.
A boy
just like you .

Like Grief

ice is treacherous. What matters
is suddenly there before you, but unclutchable.

It makes things bloom—
the weeds, the scatter of fallen branches,
the forgotten sticks poking through snow.

What went unseen before
is vibrant, important,
fragile and brief.

It astonishes,
its comforting stasis
blossoms like memory.

History is told in the dross left behind—
bejeweled skeletons of Queen Ann's lace,
the glazed face of a sunflower.

We can no longer be surefooted.
Wind curses but it doesn't touch the ice.
The snow begins as delicate seed pearls
and flowers into the poverty of empty fields.

Armour

memory cut open
pungent and sour
as milk gone bad

shock repeating
itself in rage
white hot articulation
scorching simple plans:
a picnic, a sunset walk,
supper at the kitchen table

your heart
a cold wet cave
curled into itself
secreted by brambles
guarded by wolves

and yet
someplace tender still
fetal
this naked space
where we labor to fashion
the only shield
we own

Chicken Love

She has posted herself
by the backdoor
in love and waiting.
Poking her head in the window,
she startles guests.
When he leaves the house
she hops down from her perch
to follow him around,
purling and muttering her chicken love,
telling him everything, *everything.*
This summer she was just one
fluffy chick who came in the mail.

He feeds her scraps from dinner,
sunflower seeds meant for other birds.
Come the snowstorm
he says he can't bear it
her feathers glistening with ice
snow making her a little hat
as she holds her vigil.

Cooped up with fowl company,
I imagine she dreams
of how she will stalk him,
trail him into the garden, cluck to him
at the woodpile, settle on her perch
again by the back door.
These cold February days
there is no one waiting for him
when he takes stale bread to the feeder.

I have come to think his is a roostery love
we can share. Besides, what accounts
for who loves who, who erases the sorry aches
of loneliness, who makes a place
feel like home?

For Soldier Returning

How do you hate
so much
what you did

that you volunteer
to march into it
again?

Securing the Perimeter

I

Once I loved a man
who secured
an invisible perimeter,
razor-wired shut
wandering eye on patrol.

I waited for him, hoping to dismantle
what ticked inside him
trying to navigate
the concussion of his moods,
to ignore his dereliction
of duties.

What did I know of war,
but what I tasted
on his lips?

II

If you don't tell it, maybe you didn't see it.
If you don't tell it, maybe you didn't feel it.
If you don't tell it, maybe you didn't do it.
If you don't tell it, maybe you can forget.

Maybe the war will stop living in your gut,
marching to the flat knock of your heart.

III

Who counts the bodies
after war is over?
How long does friendly
fire last? Who listens
to children crying in their beds
missing fathers
already home?

IV

He wears memories like skin--
so close we are seconds
away from the flash.

V

The dead do not need to sit at table with us;
they have their own places to be.
We might stop feeding the children
decay with every meal. And no, dear, no
wine for me, the color of blood.

VI

He lives in no woman's land, a boundary
between dying and dying. Between
our raggedness and what we planned.

VII

Were Adam and Eve this desolate?

Did they make love in the light
of the blood moon?
Did she lie awake listening
to his breathing, patrolling the shadowlands
of his dreams?

Did Adam stalk the perimeter
of the garden while Eve watched,
brushing away the scorpions
crawling toward her
in the unforgiving sun?

Recovery

He taught me silence
and the company of fear.
I learned from him
to listen to gestures.
Omens inside the house and out.
There were voices in the wind
again this morning.
No birds came to the feeder.

The image repeats:
the carelessness of his body
pressed to another woman's
as I wait voiceless
and certain in the night.

Sorrow only feeds itself
stunning the brain
stalling the heart.

I can vouch for today:
my blood flows, my eyes discern,
my voice is operative.
I am at least half alive.
But a kiss now
could only taste of grief.

I have traveled the years well-armed,
my blood dreaming rage.
I imagine him returning.
He comes to ask questions. I tell him
everything is happening as it should,
but you do not necessarily die.

No Blood

Gray feathers animated
the kitchen when I walked in.
But no corpse.

The culprit and I had a long talk—
I talked, he listened,
or appeared to while I brushed him.
I discussed instinct and urges,
pointed out how well fed he is,
acknowledged his need for the limbic:
there are squirrels to chase, chickens
to stalk and no one need be killed.
His purr vibrated my sternum,
he licked my hand.

I have my own brand of violence
I confided.
You can't yet know
how many ways
there are
to beg forgiveness.

Civil War: Greece 1947

Hungry, children roam ragged fields:
shorn heads, empty eyes, thin
legs running through seasoned grasses.
War stunned and wild the children pause in vacant lots
to build crude cages from what they scavenge, quarreling
among themselves, craving trees, shade, firewood,
a cool place to rest, a little protection.
They know fields of ravaged anemones, baked earth,
sticks and strings, the knock of delicate rib cages,
hollow bellies.

One triumphant child hoists a small found tree:
shrine of hope to the multitude who follow.
They plant the tree, smear branches
with lime and sap, and lie down in shabby
grasses, their heads bobbing like sparrows hunting seed.

Then still as rocks the children whistle calls they've listened to
in the still mornings after grenades and artillery lullabies:
plover and lark, thrush and finch.
They watch the lone tree, where a tired bird lights,
suddenly trapped by its feet
on the sticky branch. Terrified, the caught bird
wildly flaps its wings
until leaped upon by screeching children
who wring its neck.

Memoir

1

rush of memory
and no language
for what I cannot tell

2

I am a character
in my own story
the unreliable novel
I'm surprised
to have written

3

a ripened apple
beginning to perfume the room
delicious rot and a bird
fluttering against the window
the zinc-gray sky of childhood
a netted fish flapping to free itself
a small pile of clean bones.

Toward a War Poem

Notes: why do I keep imagining what I have not seen?
images like flares in the night
lodge in my brain

those who tell of war
say again and again
boredom and horror the rush of everything
beauty in strange moments
then nothingness

your bare hands
strangle of smoke
hurt of flak
blistered
siren dazed
adrenaline sharp
bullet walls
dark crimson
seared
artillery silhouettes
twisted
staccato quiet
grief you eat

Kisses

This morning I found a kiss of yours left in a coffee cup
and later, half a sticky one on the lip of the oatmeal bowl.
Yesterday there was one floating serenely
in the mud puddle next to the car
Then the one at my clavicle I noticed
when I was brushing my teeth.
I am sorry you are so casual about your affection.

I bring in roses from the garden as a sign of my regard;
I alphabetize the spices and line them up like soldiers,
carefully fold your socks, smooth your rumpled hair.

Your kisses are undisciplined, wayward.
They turn up late and early.
They tickle the back of my neck
and linger in the cup of my hand.
They wait for me on the steering wheel.

I order this wantonness to cease
before I throw you
into the brig
of my desire.

The Frail Ones

They shrivel like leaves.
Brightness evaporates, the crisp
dry edges curl inward.
Even their eyes fade
that used to see everything --
what they didn't like
and how they told me so.
The sharp tongues
slur, forget my name.
Oh, they are skittering away!
So frail now, hard to hold
without a shattering.
I would like to say I don't like this!
I would like to tell them so.

I will tell you
no one prepares us for the sudden
changing of the guard,
the relentless march: to witness
in excruciating detail
the demise of the other.
And the simple truth:
we are next, oh
we are next.

At the Airport

Try to decipher the muffled announcements
with your heart thrumming in your ears.
The unfamiliar voice could be calling you
back, urging you not to take *that* flight.

You might be distracted by people waiting,
their mouths tasting words they will use
when the loved one appears tired and tousled.
No graceful arabesque of embrace,
but an awkward seizing
and rush of clichés as people become seasoned
to one another at the mecca of baggage claim.

And the goodbyes more distracting yet:
the surreptitious, touchless clinging,
the caged bird words caught in throats and eyes,
the stall of time, or rush of it, the ambivalent eagerness
to get the tearing apart over.

Greek tragedies soap operas sitcom love poetry grief
at every turn with the beeping carts
that creep up behind you bleating
"Too much! Too much! Too much!"
and the droning voice of God announcing
what could be your departure.

Matrilineal

The way she pats dough, throws
crumbs to birds, ties hair
to snake down her back
her hands red raw.

The grace of hip and calf
at the clothesline careful
trace of red on lips
before answering the door.

Vanilla, lemon oil, vinegar, soap
spools of thread, dust cloths, thimble,
lint and string, the unpaid gas bill--

part of my lost life in her apron pockets.

Stories stirred like soup with secret
ingredients parables at dinner warnings
at bedside the same voice milking
the diurnal air lament
of mourning dove repeating, repeating
shadow by the night door
at the window eyes knitting worry.

Little white teeth
growing in her hand
as she waves goodbye.

Rapprochement

War ends. Ghosts rise up
white against
the world gone black.
Color like hope bled out.

I cannot thank you for your service--
such words stick in my throat
empty and brutal
in their way. What do I know
of your hauntings? You who ate the landscape
and estimate its poison.

A whitewash rises from darkest deeds
like the humming of patriotic tunes.
I did not do my bit, unless worry counts
and private skirmishes from another life.
Out of your duty we compute
equations of darkness whose sum
is youth consumed.

The vulture of peace
circles the math of ruin.
What we destroyed
 blinding as clean snow
—your tidy annihilation.

Requiem for the Living

It is you we mourn.
Young forever, we are done
with our wild, thirsty
natures. We do not feel,
we do not walk on prosthetic
devices. We are not widows,
or instantly aged by survival--
no dark smear of memory
or waving flags at lies.
Greeted by blessed silence,
we sleep in its sweet country.

You, the living,
need be mourned--
for what is writ in your blood
makes war possible, then necessary.
Hear us dead whispering to you--
the rasp of flies.

PATRILINEAL

I cast my father into the trees
and hear his voice in the whir
of hummingbird wings,
in the scolding winds before rain.

I cast my father into the trees
where leaves lie palm open
waiting for truth wide as sky,
where memories, like insects
live invisible lives.

I cast my father into the trees
where night is ripe for complaint
honeyed moon singing his songs
that I am doomed to remember
now only owls can hear.

I cast my father into the trees
nearby, but not too close,
where I can hear him, but not respond,
where I can relive his slow
disappearance, no longer
holding his promises in my cupped heart.

I cast my father into the trees
thinking one day
he may take flight
and all the disappointments
may then scatter
like spring blossoms
in the dark night wind
of my own demise.

Praise Song

We are tattered bits of cloth
looking for pattern
in the dependable void.

At dusk, when fevers rise
colors are more beautiful:
the day rinsed of its complaints,
weariness gentling us.

      Gray of rock or guns?
      Startle of red bird in pine
      or blood in ripe grass?
      Golden sunglitter on sand
      or dazzle of bombs?
      Blue Giotto snow or planeless sky?

      Fiery end, stars ignited in blackest night.
      Mud, bamboo, diamonds, steel,
      gold, bolts of fabric, paper and pen.
      Who is to say what is more useful
      or what feeds us best?

We have our work: stitching passion
to another's.
      Witness how well we quilt ourselves
      into something
      useful
      from singular
      desolation.

We have tools: eyes to watch, hands
to soothe, our minds to fasten to
breath, our breath to words, to curse,
to praise our ragged world.

WALKING AT DUSK ON NEW YEAR'S

Border crossing of the year:
wind sands our faces
to a ruddy glow
as we make our wooly way.

Mother of pearl
peacock night all blues and eyes.
Tail lights' ruby winks up ahead.

We hold hands, like pilgrims,
our cheeks damp with benediction
of snow and history.
Gratitude and hope taste like this.

And the sweet tipple
this night with woodsmoke comfort
and later to bed to sleep in arms
who want to hold you
to the next decade.

ELAINE HANDLEY

The impulse for this book comes out of Elaine Handley's teaching and learning from veterans. The idea of securing a perimeter is essential for people at war and extends to other groups she has worked with: prison inmates, troubled adolescents, seniors, adult college students and precocious writerly teenagers. For her, poetry explores territory on both sides of our perimeters, the tender and the harsh. Her first poetry book was *Letters to My Migraine*.

She lives in the woods outside of Saratoga Springs, NY with her husband. A professor of Writing and Literature at SUNY Empire State College, she is also on the Faculty of the NYS Young Writers Institute. Three previous collaborative chapbooks each won best book of poetry from the Adirondack Center for Writing.